MAGNETS

SCIENCE SECRETS

Jason Cooper

Rourke
Publishing LLC
Vero Beach, Florida 32964

www.rourkepublishing.com

PHOTO CREDITS: ©Lynn M. Stone: pages 4, 7, 10, , 15, 18; pages 8, 13, 17, 18 ©K-8 Images; title page Image 100 LTD; courtesy NASA, page 21.

Title page: *These magnets are a favorite with children.*

Series Editor: Henry Rasof

Cover and interior design by Nicola Stratford

Library of Congress Cataloging-in-Publication Data

Cooper, Jason, 1942-
  Magnets / Jason Cooper.
     v. cm. — (Science secrets)
Includes bibliographical references and index.
Contents: What is a magnet? — Magnetism — A magnet's poles — Earth and magnets — Magnetic rocks — Magnet shapes — Magnets at work — Magnets with electricity — Other magnets.
  ISBN 1-58952-412-8
1. Magnetism—Juvenile literature. [1. Magnetism.] I. Title. II.
     Series: Cooper, Jason, d 1942- . Science secrets.
  QC753.7 .C66 2002
  538—dc21
                                        2002015712

Printed in the USA

TABLE OF CONTENTS

What Is a Magnet?	5
Magnetism	6
A Magnet's Poles	9
Earth and Magnets	11
Magnetic Rocks	14
Magnet Shapes	16
Magnets at Work	19
Magnets with Electricity	20
Other Magnets	22
Glossary	23
Index	24
Further Reading/Websites to Visit	24

WHAT IS A MAGNET?

You've probably seen magnets. The most common ones are made of metal containing iron. Steel is such a metal. These magnets will stick to other magnets or to other metal objects containing iron. A steel paper clip will stick to a magnet.

Many people put magnets on refrigerator doors. Sometimes they are there to remind people to do certain things. Other magnets you may know about are used on doors to keep them tightly closed.

A magnet in this electric can opener holds the lid of a metal tin can.

MAGNETISM

A magnet works because of a natural force called magnetism. Magnetism is a force that you cannot see. We say it is **invisible**.

The force of magnetism pushes and pulls, causing a magnet to pull some metal objects. This may make them stick to the magnet. Magnets also can push or pull other magnets.

Each magnet has a **magnetic field** around it. This is the area where the force of magnetism can affect objects. Put a steel paper clip in the magnetic field of a magnet, and the clip will be pulled to the magnet.

Paper clips "stick" to a horseshoe magnet.

Same poles repel each other

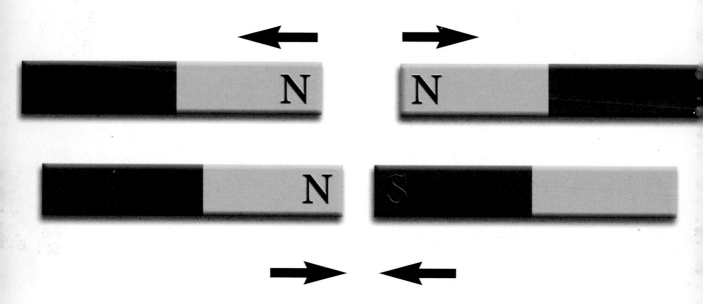

Opposite poles attract each other

A MAGNET'S POLES

One kind of magnet is a bar magnet. It is shaped like a candy bar. Its pull is more powerful at its ends, or **poles**, than in the middle.

One pole of a magnet is called the north pole. The other end is called the south pole. The north pole of one magnet will attract the south pole of another. When two north poles face each other, they will repel, or **resist**, each other. The same goes for two south poles.

MAGNETIC NORTH POLE

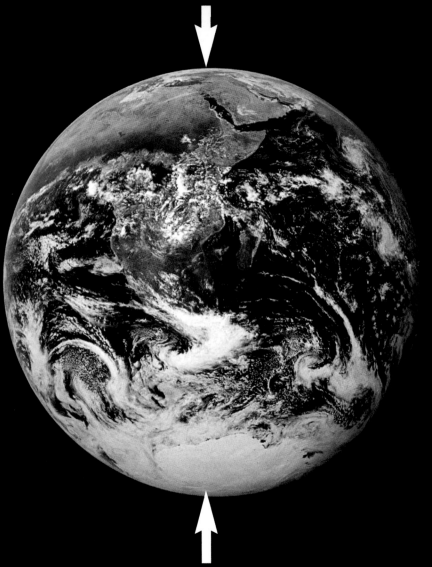

MAGNETIC SOUTH POLE

EARTH AND MAGNETS

The earth has magnetic poles, too. The earth has a center, or **core**. Many scientists believe that this core is made of magnetic materials.

The north magnetic pole is in the Arctic. The south magnetic pole is at the other end of the earth, in Antarctica. The earth's magnetic pull makes the magnetic needle of a compass line up north and south.

Like an ordinary magnet, the earth also has a magnetic field.

The earth has two magnetic poles.

An electromagnet that weighs 2,000 pounds (a little more than 900 kg)

Magnets are used in this drawing toy.

MAGNETIC ROCKS

Long ago, magnets were found only in the ground. They were "magic stones" and were called **lodestones**. No one thought these stones would stick to metal.

Today we know lodestone as **magnetite**, a type of iron. Magnetite is rough and jagged. Lodestone is magnetic by nature. That means magnetite has the pull of a magnet.

This stone has the pull of a magnet.

MAGNETS AT WORK

Magnets are used almost everywhere. We see them used in homes, factories, hospitals, laboratories, and other places. Magnets help computers, telephones, electric motors, and other devices to work.

A magnetic **compass** has a magnet inside. The magnet tells which way a person is going—north, east, south, or west.

*A compass uses a magnetic
   needle to tell directions.*

19

MAGNETS WITH ELECTRICITY

Magnets that use electricity are called **electromagnets**. Magnets like these can lift certain heavy metal objects. This kind of magnet can be turned on or off.

When the electric current is turned on, the magnet lifts the objects. But when the current is off, the objects are released.

Devices like telephones, motors, loudspeakers, and doorbells often contain electromagnets.

Electromagnets help with lifting and moving heavy things.

OTHER MAGNETS

You have learned about simple magnets that pick up steel objects and about electromagnets that make electrical devices work.

Some countries have trains powered by magnetism. The magnetic fields push or pull on the train to move it along the track. These trains can go faster than many other trains.

Materials that contain no iron can also be magnetic. Some of these are metals, and some are even gases or ceramics. The plates we eat off are a type of ceramic but are not magnetic.

Magnets are all around us.

GLOSSARY

compass (KUMP us) — an instrument that uses a magnetic needle to tell direction

core (KORE) — the center or inner part

electromagnets (ee LEK tro MAG netz) — magnets that operate by electric current and can be turned on and off

invisible (in VIZ ah bull) — unable to be seen by the naked eye

lodestones (LOAD STOHNZ) — another name for magnetite

magnetic field (mag NET ik FEELD) — the area surrounding a magnet in which the magnet's force is present

magnetism (MAG nuh tizz um) — the invisible pushing or pulling force of magnets

magnetite (MAG nuh tite) — a kind of rock, which is magnetic by nature

poles (POLZ) — the point of highest attraction, such as the opposite ends of certain types of magnets

resist (ree ZIZZT) — to repel

23

Index

compass   11, 19

core   11

electromagnets   20, 22

lodestones   14

magnetic field   6, 11, 22

magnetite   14

north pole (of a magnet)   9, 11

south pole (of a magnet)   9, 11

Further Reading

Madgwick, Wendy. *Magnetism*. Austin: Raintree Steck-Vaughn, 1999.

Bocknek, Jonathan. *The Science of Magnets*. Milwaukee: Gareth Stevens, 2000.

Parker, Steve. *Electricity*. New York: Dorling Kindersley, 2000.

Website To Visit

ippex.pppl.gov/interactive/electricity/

About The Author

Jason Cooper has written several children's book series about a variety of topics for Rourke Publishing, including *Eye to Eye with Big Cats* and *Money Power*. Cooper travels widely to gather information for his books.